CRITICAL THINKING: GRADE 3
TABLE OF CONTENTS

Critical Thinking 3, SV 6214-8

TEACHER INTRODUCTION

Overview

Steck-Vaughn Critical Thinking is a program designed to teach thinking skills. The skills are organized according to Benjamin Bloom's *Taxonomy of Educational Objectives.** These skills include some of the seven intelligences from the theory of multiple intelligences, such as linguistic, spatial, and logical-mathematical. Pupils are taught skills that have been identified as being particularly helpful in developing four stages of thinking – Knowledge, Comprehension, Application, and Analysis. At grades 3, 4, and 5, pupils move into the higher level skills of Synthesis and Evaluation.

Program Philosophy

Direct teaching of thinking skills provides pupils with the opportunity to focus on **thinking** rather than on specific content. Practicing these skills will enable students to develop strategies which will enhance their ability to do well, not only on standardized tests, but also in real-life situations.

Pupils who have had the opportunity to practice skills are better able to transfer them to other areas of the curriculum. *Steck-Vaughn Critical Thinking* contains practice pages for every skill presented in the program. Pupils need to know whether or not they are on the right track when they are practicing a new skill. Without feedback, a pupil might continue to practice a skill incorrectly. This program encourages the use of feedback and discussion to help students "think about their thinking."

After pupils begin to consider themselves "thinkers," they will be better able to learn and make use of content area material. Practicing skills such as identifying main ideas, classifying, identifying relationships, thinking about what will happen, and inferring will help students become better readers in the content areas.

Cognitive Skills

The first unit of study is **Knowledge**. This level is considered by many educators to be the first stage in cognitive development. This starting point includes both the acquisition of information and the ability to recall information when needed. The following skills are helpful in developing this stage:

1. Classifying
2. Discriminating Between Real and Make-Believe
3. Discriminating Between Fact and Opinion
4. Discriminating Between Definition and Example
5. Outlining and Summarizing

The second unit of study is **Comprehension**. Comprehension refers to the basic level of understanding and involves the ability to know what is being communicated in order to make use of the information. This includes translating or interpreting a communication or extrapolating information from a communication. The following skills are helpful in developing this stage:

1. Comparing and Contrasting
2. Identifying Structure
3. Identifying Steps in a Process
4. Understanding Pictures
5. Comparing Word Meanings
6. Identifying Main Ideas
7. Identifying Relationships

The third unit of study is **Application**. Application is the ability to use a learned skill in a new situation. The following skills are helpful in developing this stage:

1. Ordering Objects
2. Estimating
3. Thinking About What Will Happen
4. Inferring
5. Interpreting Changes in Word Meanings

The fourth unit of study is **Analysis**. Analysis is the ability to break down information into its integral parts and to identify the relationship of each part to the total organization. The following skills are helpful in developing this stage:

1. Judging Completeness
2. Thinking About Facts That Fit
3. Distinguishing Abstract from Concrete
4. Judging Logic of Actions
5. Identifying Parts of a Story
6. Examining Story Logic
7. Recognizing True and False

The fifth unit of study in **Synthesis**. Synthesis is the ability to combine existing elements in order to create something original. The following skills are helpful in developing this stage:

1. Communicating Ideas
2. Planning Projects
3. Building Hypotheses
4. Drawing Conclusions
5. Proposing Alternatives

The sixth unit of study is **Evaluation**. Evaluation involves the ability to make a judgment about the value of something by using a standard. The following skills are helpful in developing this stage:

1. Testing Generalizations
2. Developing Criteria
3. Judging Accuracy
4. Making Decisions
5. Identifying Values
6. Interpreting the Mood of a Story

Features of the Program
Specific skills are listed in the Table of Contents and may be easily found if you need to access a certain skill or area. Each of the 35 skills has been correlated to the content areas of language arts, social studies, science, and math. This chart is on page 4. A Letter to Parents explaining the goals and benefits of the program is provided on page 5.

The Assessment Test on pages 6-7 may be used to gauge pupils' critical thinking abilities before and after completion of the program. Each unit is also followed by a two-page Assessment Test. The Student Mastery Checklist on page 8 will facilitate your record keeping.

* Bloom, Benjamin. *Taxonomy of Educational Objectives, Handbook 1: Cognitive Domain*. New York: David McKay Company, Inc., 1956.

CORRELATION TO CONTENT AREA CHART

Pages	Reading and Language Arts	Social Studies	Science	Math
9-11	✔	✔		✔
12-13	✔			
14-15	✔			
16-17		✔	✔	
18-19		✔	✔	
22-23	✔	✔		
24-25	✔			
26-27		✔	✔	
28-29		✔		✔
30-31	✔			
32-34	✔	✔	✔	
35-36	✔			
39-40	✔			✔
41-42				✔
43-44	✔			
45-46	✔			
47-48	✔			
51-52	✔			✔
53-54	✔			
55-56	✔	✔		
57-58	✔			
59-60	✔			
61-62	✔			
63-64	✔			
67-69		✔		✔
70-71	✔		✔	
72-74	✔			
75-76	✔		✔	
77-78		✔		
81-82	✔			
83-84		✔	✔	
85-86		✔		
87-88	✔			
89-90	✔			
91-92	✔			

Critical Thinking 3, SV 6214-8

Dear Parent,

Being able to think clearly and process information in increasingly complex ways is a necessity in the modern world and one of the primary goals of education. This year your child will be using critical thinking exercises to extend his or her ability to read, think, and reason.

The skills we will be practicing are grouped in levels of thinking. These levels are knowledge, comprehension, application, analysis, synthesis, and evaluation. The levels are each important. The higher the level of thinking, the more complex the task is. The exercises move from the concrete to the more abstract levels of thinking. We will practice skills such as classifying, identifying main ideas, inferring, and judging completeness.

From time to time, your child may bring home some of these critical thinking practice sheets. To best help your child, please consider the following suggestions:

- Provide a quiet place to work.
- Go over the directions together.
- Show interest in the work.
- Encourage your child to do his or her best.
- Help your child if he or she gets frustrated.
- Check the lesson when it is complete.

Many of these exercises can be easily extended by thinking of similar examples. Your involvement will encourage your child, give you information about how he or she thinks, and provide an opportunity for you to work together. Positive family experiences such as these help promote life-long learning.

Thanks for your help!

Sincerely,

Name _____ Date _____

Assessment Test

A. Judging Completeness

Look at the picture of an antique store window. Some of the items in the window have missing parts. In the sentences below, circle the word that tells what is needed to complete each item.

1. The clock needs   legs   hands   eyes.

2. The wagon needs   wheels   windows   doors.

3. The television needs a   handle   screen   frame.

4. The silverware chest is missing   forks   spoons   knives.

5. The chair needs   legs   wheels   sheets.

B. Relevance of Information

Pretend that the items pictured above are complete. Write the name of the item you would use for each task.

1. to set the table for dinner _____

2. to sit at a desk to do homework _____

3. to take home many bags of groceries _____

4. to get to school on time _____

5. to get the latest news report _____

Critical Thinking 3, SV 6214-8

Assessment Test

C.   Communicating Ideas

The Mayans lived many hundreds of years ago. The symbol on the right is a number from their writing system. Each bar stands for **5**. Each dot stands for **1**. So this symbol means **12**. The chart below should show symbols for the numbers **1** to **20**. Use Mayan symbols to fill in the missing numbers.

•	• •		• • • •
___		• • ___	• • • • ___
		• ═══	
• • • ═══	• • • • ═══		• ═══
		• • • • ═══	

D.   Changes in Word Meanings
Inferring

The sentences give clues to the meanings of the underlined words. Write what you think each underlined word means.

1. I will give you a <u>ring</u> when I get home from school. If you don't hear from me, please call. _____

2. At lunchtime there is usually a long <u>line</u> at the delicatessen. _____

3. I can't find my other <u>sock</u> and shoe. _____

4. The teacher calls the <u>roll</u> at the beginning of each school day. _____

Student Mastery Checklist

Skill #

Name	1	2	3	4	5	6	7	8	9	10	11	12	13	14	15	16	17	18	19	20	21	22	23	24	25	26	27	28	29	30	31	32	33	34	35

Critical Thinking 3, SV 6214-8

UNIT 1 Knowledge
Classifying

The words in each word web name things in a group. Choose a word from the box below that describes the group. Write the word to finish the web. The first one is done for you.

jewels	furniture	relatives
tools	sports	clothes

1. emerald   diamond

   jewels

   sapphire   ruby

2. cousin   aunt

   _____

   uncle   sister

3. jacket   pants

   _____

   socks   shirt

4. chair   bed

   _____

   table   desk

5. wrench   pliers

   _____

   hammer   saw

6. bowling   tennis

   _____

   soccer   baseball

Critical Thinking 3, SV 6214-8   **9**

Classifying

Imagine that you have four cookbooks about different foods. Next to each cookbook, write the names of four foods that might be in that book's recipes. Use the food names in the box.

hot dogs	broccoli	apples	shrimp
turkey	potatoes	perch	tuna
peaches	salmon	watermelon	chicken
corn	cherries	beef	carrots

1.

_____

_____

_____

_____

3.

_____

_____

_____

_____

2.

_____

_____

_____

_____

4.

_____

_____

_____

_____

Critical Thinking 3, SV 6214-8

Classifying

Use the words in the box to fill in each blank. Write your own answer for the second part of number 4.

equal   triangles   squares   rectangles   circles   three   four

a   b   c   d

e   f   g   h

1. Figures **e** and **g** are _____ .

   Each has _____ sides.

2. **a** and **d** are _____ .

   They have _____ sides.

3. **b** and **h** are _____ .

   They have four _____ sides.

4. **c** and **f** are _____ .

   How many sides do they have?_____

   _____

Real and Fanciful

A. Put **R** before each name of a real person. Put **F** before each name of a fanciful or make-believe being.

1. ____ genie   5. ____ troll   9. ____ electrician

2. ____ farmer   6. ____ teacher   10. ____ elf

3. ____ ghost   7. ____ plumber   11. ____ monster

4. ____ lawyer   8. ____ painter   12. ____ leprechaun

B. Fanciful beings may be used in a sentence about something that could really happen. Mark each sentence **R** for real or **F** for fanciful.

____ 1. The child wrote a story about a ghost.

____ 2. Della played with an elf after school.

____ 3. There are many movies about monsters.

____ 4. Children dressed up as leprechauns on Halloween.

____ 5. A troll got into our pond and made a great deal of trouble.

____ 6. The genie granted my wish for a new bicycle.

C. 1. Write your own sentence about something fanciful or make-believe.

_____

_____

2. Write a sentence that tells about something that could really happen.

_____

_____

    Critical Thinking 3, SV 6214-8

Real and Fanciful

A. Here are two books about horses.
Book **X** tells real things about horses.
Book **Y** is a fairy tale. It tells about
things that horses really could not be
or do. Look at the sentences below.
On the line, write the letter of the
book in which you would expect to
read the sentence.

X

1. _____ Horses like to eat hay.

2. _____ Horses are purple.

3. _____ Horses have four legs.

4. _____ Horses can talk.

5. _____ Horses wear socks.

6. _____ Horses are good pets.

7. _____ Horses can shop.

8. _____ Horses fix supper.

Y

B. 1. Write a sentence that tells something a horse can really do.

_____

_____

2. Write a fanciful sentence about a horse.

_____

_____

Name _____ Date _____

Fact and Opinion

A **fact** can be proved to be true. An **opinion** tells only what someone thinks or believes.

Fact:
Two plus two equals four.

Opinion:
Four is a lucky number.

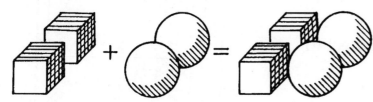 

Read each sentence below. Put **F** before each fact and **O** before each opinion.

_____ 1. Softball is the best game to play.

_____ 2. Leon came into class after the bell rang.

_____ 3. Winter is the most enjoyable season of the year.

_____ 4. Some horses live on the plains.

_____ 5. January is a good month to have a birthday.

_____ 6. A meter is smaller than a mile.

_____ 7. Sunday is the first day of the week.

_____ 8. The earth is over two hundred years old.

_____ 9. It is more important to be kind than to be honest.

_____ 10. Brazil is the most beautiful country in the world.

_____ 11. Alaska is the largest state in the United States.

_____ 12. Toronto is a great place to visit.

_____ 13. Dogs are better pets than cats.

_____ 14. Snakes and lizards are both reptiles.

 Critical Thinking 3, SV 6214-8

Name _____   Date _____

Fact and Opinion

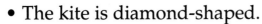

A. The picture shows a kite. Below are some statements of fact about the kite. Write two sentences of your own about the kite that state facts.

- The kite is diamond-shaped.
- The kite is made of paper and light wood.
- The kite has a design on it.

1. _____

    _____

    _____

2. _____

    _____

B. These sentences state some opinions about the kite. Write two more sentences that tell your opinions about kites.

- The kite is a delightful toy.
- The kite is flying very gracefully.
- Diamond-shaped kites are better than box kites.

1. _____

    _____

2. _____

    _____

Critical Thinking 3, SV 6214-8

·⁻ ⁻ ·Definition and Example· ⁻ ·

> When you give the meaning of a word, you give its **definition**. For example, a **mammal** is a warm-blooded animal that has hair, lungs, and a backbone.

> When you name things that belong to a group, you give **examples**. For instance, **cows, dogs, mice,** and **apes** are mammals.

Each sentence gives either a definition or an example. If it gives a definition, put **D** after the sentence. If it gives an example, put **E** after the sentence.

1. A reptile is a cold-blooded animal that crawls or creeps. _____

2. Evergreen trees are trees such as pines, firs, and redwoods. _____

3. A kangaroo is a mammal that has small front legs and large

   hind legs. _____

4. Iron, gold, silver, and tin are metals. _____

5. Bats are mammals that hang upside down during the day. _____

6. An island is a piece of land surrounded by water. _____

7. Beavers are mammals that build dams. _____

8. Notions are things such as needles, pins, snaps, and buttons. _____

9. A container is an object used for holding or carrying things. _____

10. Some islands of the Pacific are Fiji, the Solomon Islands, and

    New Caledonia. _____

Name _____ **Date** _____

Definition and Example

For each puzzle, a definition and examples are provided. Use the definition and examples to figure out the word. Write it in the puzzle. The first one is done for you.

Heavenly body that orbits the sun

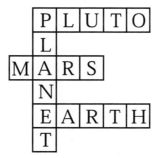

1. Large towns where people live and work

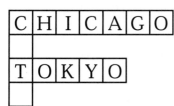

4. Something played for fun

2. The blossom of a plant

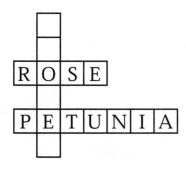

5. Tall plant with a trunk and leaves

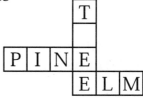

3. One of the twelve periods of time making up a year

	M	A	Y
J	U	N	E

6. Sweet food served at the end of a meal

P	U	D	D	I	N	G

B	R	O	W	N	I	E	S

Outlining and Summarizing

A **summary** sums up or tells briefly what a paragraph or story is about. A summary tells the main facts or ideas. It does not give all the details.

Read the paragraph below. Then use the word box to complete the summary that follows.

Sea life is often divided into three groups: plankton, animals that swim, and plants and animals that live on the sea's floor. Plankton include tiny plants and animals that drift through the sea in large groups. Plant plankton are important because they make oxygen, a gas needed by all animals. The animals that swim include fish, whales, turtles, and octopuses. These swimming animals are mostly hunters. They eat other fish for food. Usually, big fish eat little fish. However, huge whales eat tiny plankton. Many plants and animals live only at the bottom of the sea. In this group are crabs, lobsters, snails, coral, and sponges. Many of these animals eat plankton, and many are food themselves for the swimmers of the sea.

crabs	floor	sea	smaller
plankton	animal	float	sponges

Life in the _____ includes _____ , swimmers, and

plants and animals that live on the ocean _____ . Plankton are

tiny plants and animals that do not swim but _____ . The

swimmers include any sea _____ that swims, and the bottom

dwellers include _____ , _____ , and coral. Most sea

animals feed on _____ fish or plants.

Outlining and Summarizing

Read each paragraph below. Find the words that tell what the paragraph is about. We call these words the **main idea**. Write the main idea on the line below the title. The first word has been written for you. Now write the facts from the paragraph on the lines below the main idea.

There are many names for homes. A palace is a large home for a ruler to live in. A mansion is smaller than a palace. A house is where a family often lives. A cottage is a very small house of wood or stone.

Homes

★ ___Many_____

A. _____

B. _____

C. _____

D. _____

Seeds travel in many ways. Birds drop them. Winds carry them. Insects bring seeds on their feet. Seeds stick to animals' fur and are moved along. Some seeds fall to the ground from bushes and trees.

Seeds

★ _____

A. _____

B. _____

C. _____

D. _____

E. _____

Name _____   Date _____

Unit 1
Assessment Test

A.   Real and Fanciful

Read each pair of sentences. Write **R** if the sentence tells about something that could happen. Write **F** if it tells about something fanciful.

1. _____   The tiny <u>elves</u> quickly made boots.

   _____   That <u>shoemaker</u> carefully fixed my old shoes.

2. _____   An <u>eagle</u> soared high into the sky.

   _____   The <u>unicorn</u> flew into the clouds.

3. _____   A <u>leprechaun</u> buried the pot of gold.

   _____   The <u>miner</u> worked underground searching for diamonds.

B.   Classifying
Outlining and Summarizing

Read the underlined words in the sentences above. Decide whether each word names something real or something fanciful. Write each word under the correct main idea in the outline below.

I. Fanciful

   A. _____

   B. _____

   C. _____

II. Real

   A. _____

   B. _____

   C. _____

Critical Thinking 3, SV 6214-8

Assessment Test (p. 2)

C. Definition and Example

The picture shows three floors of a store. The definitions on the left tell what kind of thing you can find on each floor. Under each definition, write the correct word from the box. Then study the sign to find examples of each definition. Write the examples on the lines at the right to show on which floor you would find them.

Third Floor things for a bed 1. _____		_____ _____
Second Floor things used for serving food 2. _____		_____ _____
First Floor covering for the feet 3. _____		_____ _____

dishes
footwear
bedding

plate   bowl   shoes   blanket
pillow   saucer   quilt   sheet
cup   boots   slippers   sandals
mattress   platter

D. Fact and Opinion

Complete the two parts of the sentence to make it tell your opinion.

The best floor in the store is the _____ because _____

_____ .

Name _____   Date _____

UNIT 2 Comprehension
Comparing and Contrasting

1. Circle the things that are found on a playground.

   diving board   swings   seesaw   slide

2. Circle the things that are alive.

   babies   flowers   rocks   sand

3. Circle the things that are hard to break.

   iron   butter   bricks   crackers   concrete

4. Circle the animals that live on land.

   goats   fish   horses   camels   whales

5. Circle the things that you might fill with air.

   balloon   wall   football   tire   pool

6. Circle the things that you can drink.

   milk   crackers   water   juice   bread

7. Circle the things that are heavy to lift.

   elephant   truck   kite   stove   TV

8. Circle the things that can make a loud noise.

   firecracker   sponge   horn   drum   mop

                    Critical Thinking 3, SV 6214-8

·Comparing and Contrasting

A. Read each sentence. Then underline the statement that tells how the three things are alike.

1. How are dolphins, parrots, and dogs alike?
   a. They are all house pets.
   b. They are all animals.
   c. They all have feet.

2. How are staples, paper clips, and rubber bands alike?
   a. They are all made of shiny metal.
   b. They can all be stretched to different sizes.
   c. They are all used to hold things together.

3. How are books, magazines, and newspapers alike?
   a. They all have hard covers.
   b. They all have printed words in them.
   c. They are all sold at newsstands.

4. How are plums, peaches, and cherries alike?
   a. They all have fuzzy skins.
   b. They all have pits.
   c. They are all the same size.

B. Write a sentence that tells how the items in each group are alike.

1. knife, fork, spoon

   _____

2. curtains, shades, shutters

   _____

Identifying Structure

All letters have the same kind of plan. This plan shows the parts of a letter. Use the plan to fill in the blanks in the paragraph about letters.

heading —————————————→ 5311 Foster St.
Vancouver, B.C. V6T1Z4
October 25, 1998

inside address ————→ Blazing Rocket Toy Co.
5311 Solar Lane
Anaheim, CA 92805

salutation ————→ Dear Sir or Madam:

body ————→ Six weeks ago I ordered two Deep Space Rocket Probes. I enclosed one dollar and two proof-of-purchase seals from Astro-Power cereal. I received only one Probe. Please send me another Probe. I will be watching my mailbox for it.

close —————————————→ Sincerely,

Carlos Peña

signature —————————————→ Carlos Peña

Letters have parts that appear in order. They begin with the writer's address and date, which is called the _____. They end with the writer's _____. The _____, which appears after the heading, gives the name of the person receiving the letter. The _____ greets the person or company to whom the letter is addressed. The writer's message is contained in the _____. The brief good-bye following the body is called the _____.

Identifying Structure

A. Stories, pictures, music, and many other things follow a plan. Look at the plan for these two lines of music. They are the same except for two notes in each line. Circle the notes where the plan of the music is different.

B. Most stories have the same kind of plan. Of course, the words are different. This drawing shows a story's plan. Fill in the blanks in the story with the words that fit.

1. beginning
2. characters
3. time
4. place

5. things happen

6. exciting point

7. problem is solved

8. ends

A story has a _____. This often tells you who the

_____ are. It usually gives the _____ and

the _____ . Then _____ . The story

reaches an _____ . Finally, the _____ ,

and the story _____ .

Name _____ Date _____

Steps in a Process

A. Put the following steps in order. Write **1** on the line before the first step in each group. Number the rest until the last step has a **4** before it.

1. Washing Dishes

   _____ Wash the dishes.

   _____ Dry the dishes.

   _____ Fill the sink with water.

   _____ Put away the dishes.

2. Getting Ready for School

   _____ Leave home.

   _____ Eat and get dressed.

   _____ Board the school bus.

   _____ Get up.

3. Making a Model Airplane

   _____ Display the finished model.

   _____ Gather the materials.

   _____ Paint the assembled model.

   _____ Put together the model.

4. Baking a Cake

   _____ Mix the ingredients.

   _____ Bake the cake.

   _____ Gather the ingredients.

   _____ Frost the cake.

B. What steps do you follow when you make a peanut butter and jelly sandwich? Write the steps below. Number the steps beginning with **1**.

_____

_____

_____

_____

_____

_____

Critical Thinking 3, SV 6214-8

Name _____   Date _____

Steps in a Process

A. Read the directions for wrapping a present. Then number the sentences from **1** to **5** to show the correct order of the steps.

Wrapping a Present

To wrap a present you must first gather the materials. You will need a gift, a box to hold the gift, wrapping paper, tape, and ribbon. Place the gift in the box. Spread out the wrapping paper and, in the center, place the box containing the gift. Neatly fold the wrapping paper around the box and smooth out all wrinkles. Then tape the paper into place. Finally, tie a ribbon around the box and add a bow.

_____ Put the gift into the box.

_____ Fold the paper around the box.

_____ Tape the paper.

_____ Put a ribbon and a bow on the wrapped box.

_____ Gather the necessary materials.

B. Read the paragraph. Then number the pictures from **1** to **4** to show the correct order of the steps in a frog's life.

A Frog's Life

A frog begins its life as a small egg in winter. A tadpole, which looks like a little fish, emerges when the egg hatches. The tadpole changes as it grows. It develops legs and lungs, and it loses its gills. Finally, a little frog with a tiny tail emerges from the water to live on land.

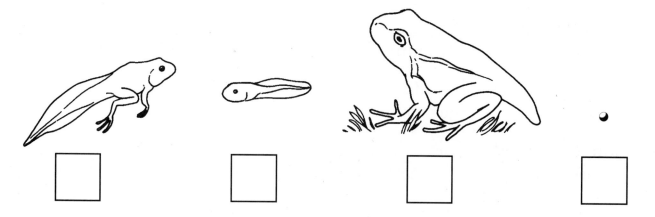

Figural Relationships

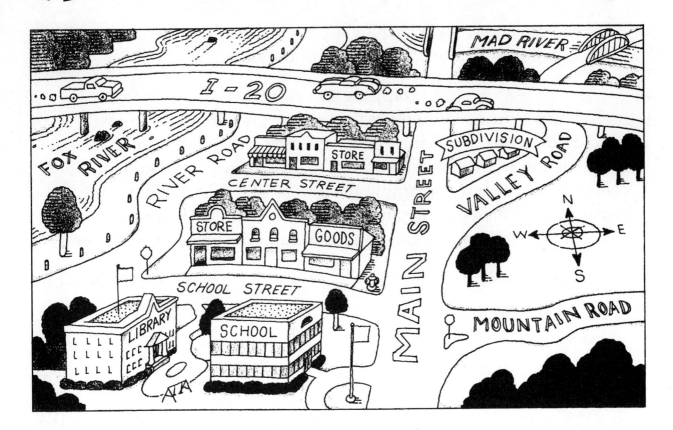

Write the word (or words) in the blank that completes each sentence.
Use the map to find your answers.

1. Route 20 crosses _____ .
      Mad River   Fox River   no river

2. The school is _____ .
     near the library   on Route 20   near the subdivision

3. People shop on _____ .
     Center Street   Mountain Road   Valley Road

4. The subdivision is closest to _____ .
     the library   the stores   Valley Road

5. Main Street runs _____ .
     north and south   east and west

Figural Relationships

You can find many squares, rectangles, and triangles in the figure below. Some of the shapes are not easy to find. First, find all the squares and write the number on the line below. Next, find all the rectangles. Finally, find the triangles. You might use three different colors of crayons to trace the three different kinds of shapes.

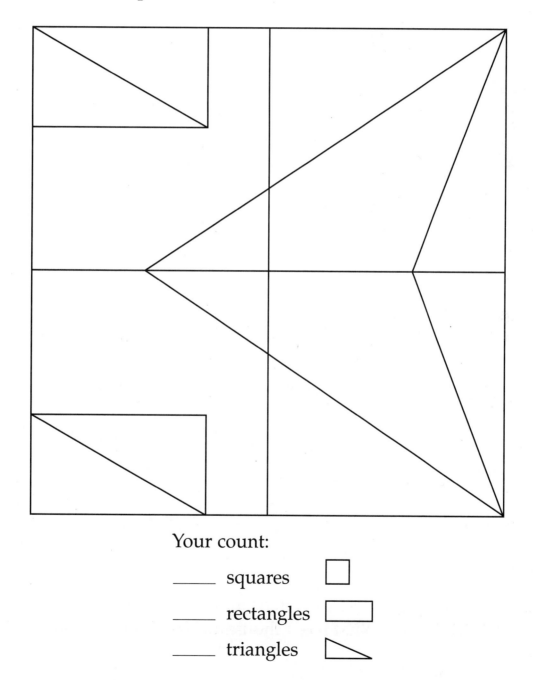

Your count:

_____ squares ☐

_____ rectangles ▭

_____ triangles ◺

Name _____ Date _____

Comparing Word Meanings

A. Write a word from the box below that means the same as each word shown.

tired	build	help	afraid	under

1. scared   ___ ___ [ ] ___ ___ ___

2. construct   ___ [ ] ___ ___ ___

3. assist   ___ ___ [ ] ___

4. beneath   ___ ___ ___ [ ] ___

5. exhausted   ___ ___ [ ] ___ ___ ___

Write the letters from the boxes in order to finish the answer to this riddle.

Riddle: When is a piece of wood like a king?

Answer: When it's a [ ] [ ] [ ] [ ] [ ]

B. Write a word from the box below that is the opposite of each word shown.

wrong	seldom	small	arrive

1. leave   [ ] ___ ___ ___ ___ ___

2. often   [ ] ___ ___ ___ ___ ___

3. enormous   ___ ___ [ ] ___ ___

4. right   [ ] ___ ___ ___ ___

Write the letters from the boxes in order to answer this riddle.

Riddle: What has a thousand teeth but no mouth?

Answer: [ ] [ ] [ ] [ ]

© Steck-Vaughn Company   Critical Thinking 3, SV 6214-8

Comparing Word Meanings

Read the story. Then follow the directions to complete parts **A** and **B**.

A Fanciful Tale

The hike was almost over. Tom, Tim, and Tina were looking forward to leaving the woods. Their legs were weary. Their backpacks seemed heavy.

"Oh," Tom exclaimed, "I'll be glad to take off this backpack!"

"Good," buzzed a mosquito. "Let's see what you have left to eat."

"Nothing for you," said Tom crossly. He slapped at the pesky mosquito.

"You're rude," said the mosquito, dodging Tom's hand. And it bit Tom on the nose.

A. Use a word from the story to complete these sentences.

1. Another word for **tired** is _____.

2. The insect named in the story is a _____.

3. When Tom spoke **angrily**, he spoke _____.

4. Tom was told he was impolite, or _____.

5. The bug avoided Tom's hand by _____ it.

B. Use a word from the box to complete these sentences.

entertaining	annoying	imaginary	hit	weighty

1. **Fanciful** means _____.

2. Another word for **heavy** is _____.

3. When Tom slapped at the bug, he tried to _____ it.

4. The insect was _____ Tom.

5. A story like this is _____, but not true.

Critical Thinking 3, SV 6214-8

Name _____   Date _____

Identifying Main Ideas

Read each paragraph. Copy the items in the box to fill in the main idea and details of the paragraph.

1. Honeybees are insects that produce honey, a food eaten by humans. The wax from their honeycombs is used to make useful things such as candles. Bees fertilize plants as they fly from flower to flower. Honeybees are very helpful to people.

Bees make honey.	Bees fertilize flowers.
Beeswax is used to make useful things.	Honeybees help people.

Main Idea: _____

Details: a. _____

           b. _____

           c. _____

2. Despite the cold, there is much to do outside in the winter. Some people ice-skate on frozen ponds. Others go sledding down snow-covered hills. Many go cross-country and downhill skiing.

go skiing things to do outside in winter	ice-skate on ponds sled down hills	

Main Idea: _____

Details: a. _____

           b. _____

           c. _____

                                     Critical Thinking 3, SV 6214-8

Identifying Main Ideas

The **main idea** tells what a story is about. Circle one sentence in each story that gives the main idea. Draw a line through any sentence that does not belong in the story.

1. Ants build many kinds of nests. Some dig tunnels in the earth and pile dirt above the ground. Termites also burrow. Some ants live in hollow trees. Other ants use sticky leaves to build nests.

2. Babies cry to tell us something. They cry when they are hungry. They cry when they are hurt or afraid. They cry when they have wet diapers. It is fun to play with dolls.

3. Most birds build their nests in the branches of trees. Other animals live in trees, too. Some birds build their nests along the gutters of buildings. Birds have even been known to build nests on jungle gyms in playgrounds. You never know where you'll find a bird nest!

4. Watches come in many different styles. Some watches are digital, while others have regular clock faces. Many watches tell the date as well as the time. Today is September 2. There are sport watches, dressy watches, and all sorts of "fun" watches.

5. Checkers is a good indoor game, and hopscotch is a good outdoor game. As you can tell, games can be played both indoors and out. Most board games are played indoors. So are card games. Outdoor games include those that use balls and involve running. Bicycling is fun outdoors, too.

Name _____ Date _____

Identifying Main Ideas

Read each story. Circle the title below it that best states the main idea.

1. One of the most common kinds of boats on a river is the barge. It is a long, low boat with a flat bottom. Barges are used to carry heavy things such as logs, sand, and cement. Most barges do not have their own engines. Instead, they are pushed by strong tugboats.

River Traffic   Learning About Barges   How Tugboats Work

2. No harbor is complete without buoys. Buoys are floating objects that help sailors and boaters steer safely through the tricky waters near shore. Some buoys show that the water is too shallow for boats. Others warn of rocks or mark the path a boat should follow. Buoys may have bells, whistles, or flashing lights.

Bells and Whistles   Harbor Helpers   Floating Objects

3. A houseboat is built more for living than for sailing. Most houseboats are tied up at docks in calm waters. Although some people in North America live on houseboats, they are in much greater use in Asia. In places such as Hong Kong, where land is scarce, thousands of people live on houseboats.

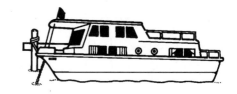

Houseboats in Asia   Sailing on Houseboats   Facts About Houseboats

                    Critical Thinking 3, SV 6214-8

Identifying Relationships

A. This lesson is just for fun. Use the letters of the alphabet in place of words. The first one is done for you.

A   B   C   D   E   F

1. an insect   __B__

2. another word for ocean   _____

G   H   I   J   K   L

3. girl's name   _____

4. a part of your face   _____

5. a blue bird   _____

M   N   O   P   Q   R

6. a word that shows surprise   _____

7. a vegetable   _____

S   T   U   V   W   X   Y   Z

8. a kind of drink   _____

9. yourself   _____

10. a word that asks a question   _____

B. In the sentences below, use letters in place of the words.

1. Oh, I see you.   __O I C U__

2. Be seein' you.   _____

3. Are you okay?   _____

Name _____ Date _____

·‑ ~Identifying Relationships· ~ ‑ ·

Rules: 1. Share with other people.
2. Do not rush into the street without looking.
3. Wash your hands before you eat.
4. Do not play with matches.
5. Obey your parents.

At the top of the page are some rules. Some short stories are below.
Write the number of the rule before the story it matches.

_____   Lupe got two sets of paints for her birthday. She really needed
only one, so she asked Mark if he would like to use one, too.

_____   Lee watched his baby brother playing on the floor. Suddenly, Lee
jumped up and quickly picked something off the floor. He put a
book of matches safely away in a drawer.

_____   Jeff sometimes forgot the good health rules his mother had taught
him. Although she often tired of reminding him, she did not give up.
One night Jeff found a washcloth instead of a napkin at his place at
the dinner table.

_____   Wendy asked Jill to stop at the card store with her after school one
day. Although Jill wanted to buy a card too, she remembered that
her parents had told her to come right home from school and not
stop anywhere else.

_____   Spring seemed a long time coming. Sue was eager to play baseball
after school. The first really warm day, she dashed out of school and
raced across the street.

Unit 2

Assessment Test

A. **Identifying Main Ideas**
Comparing Word Meanings
Identifying Figural Relationships

Read the paragraph and study the map. Use the information in the paragraph and the map to answer the questions.

Washington, D.C., has many places to visit. The White House is the home of the President of the United States. It is toured by over a million people every year. The Capitol is where Congress meets. The towering Washington Monument offers visitors a spectacular view from its top.

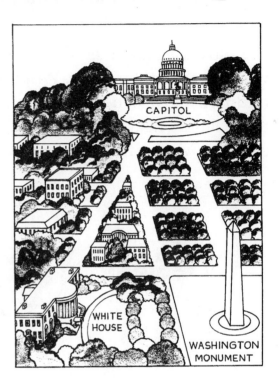

1. What is the main idea of the paragraph?

_____

2. Which place to visit is farther from the Washington Monument?

_____

3. Which word in the paragraph is another word for *outstanding*?

_____

B. **Identifying Relationships**

Circle the words a visitor could use to tell about a trip to the city of Washington, D.C.

tracks   beautiful   interesting   historic   shoe

Critical Thinking 3, SV 6214-8   **37**

Assessment Test (p. 2)

C. Comparing and Contrasting
Identifying Structure

Study the snowmen carefully. Find the **one** snowman that is missing what all the others have. Write down that snowman's letter next to 1. Next, find **two** snowmen that are missing what the others have. Write down those letters next to 2. Last, find **three** snowmen that are missing what the other snowman has. (You will write some letters more than once.)

1. _____   2. _____   3. _____

A   B   C   D

D. Identifying Steps in a Process

Choose one of the snowmen above. Write 5 steps to follow to make that snowman.

1. _____

2. _____

3. _____

4. _____

5. _____

Name _____ Date _____

Unit 3 Application
Ordering Objects

Put each list of things in order. Write **1**, **2**, **3**, and **4** to show the correct order.

I. Put the things in list A in order from short to long. Do the same for list B.

A. _____ needle   B. _____ twig

    _____ ruler   _____ sidewalk

    _____ pencil   _____ wagon

    _____ tack   _____ rake

II. Put the things in list C in order from small to large. Do the same for list D.

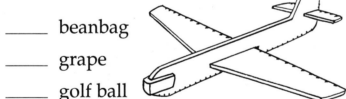

C. _____ beanbag   D._____ glider

    _____ grape   _____ robin

    _____ golf ball   _____ kite

    _____ bowling ball   _____ airplane

III. Put the things in list E in order from easy work to hard work. Do the same for list F.

E. _____ doing math   F. _____ washing dishes

    _____ writing words   _____ making beds

    _____ reading   _____ sweeping floors

    _____ singing   _____ emptying trash

Critical Thinking 3, SV 6214-8

Ordering Objects

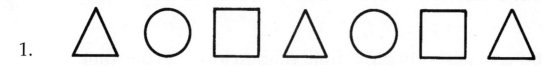

Study the figures in each group. Find the pattern, and then draw or write the figure that should come next in the pattern.

1. △ ○ □ △ ○ □ △

2. ‖‖ ‖ ‖‖‖ ⫶ ‖‖‖ ‖ ‖‖‖

3. figures row

4. Z Y X W V U T

5. squares row

6. 3 6 ★ 12 15 ★ 21

7. figures row

8. figures row

9. circles row

10. 1×1 $1 + 1$ 1×3 $1 + 3$ 1×5

Critical Thinking 3, SV 6214-8

Name _____ Date _____

Estimating

A. Put a check before the activity in each pair that you could probably do faster.

1. _____ brush your teeth   2. _____ paint the house

    _____ sharpen a pencil   _____ wash the windows

3. _____ play a game of checkers   4. _____ go swimming

    _____ take out the trash   _____ take a trip to Canada

5. _____ feed the dog   6. _____ clean your room

    _____ rake leaves in the yard   _____ eat a cookie

B. Which of the three answers below each question is closest to being correct? Put a check before the answer you choose.

1. It takes you two minutes to run around the block. How many minutes will it take you to walk around the block?

    _____ twenty   _____ two   _____ ten

2. How long does it take you to tie your shoe?

    _____ one hour   _____ ten minutes   _____ half a minute

3. How long does it take you to take a bath?

    _____ four seconds   _____ fifteen minutes   _____ two hours

4. You can put ten cookies into this box. How many can you put into this box?

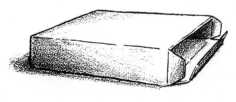 

    _____ two   _____ twelve   _____ twenty

Estimating

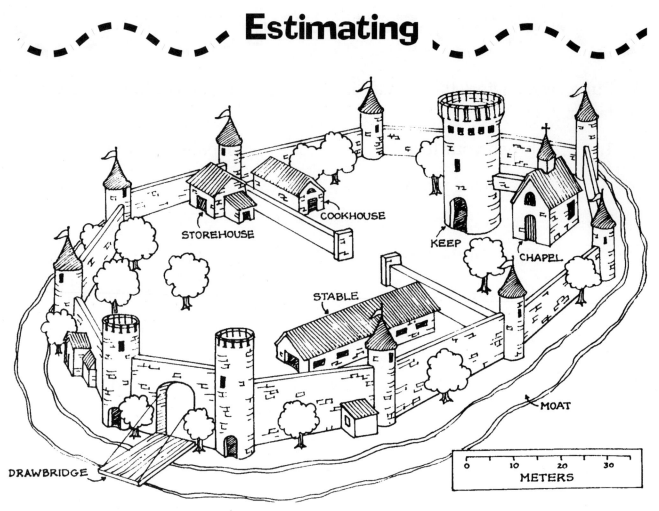

This map shows a castle or fort from the Middle Ages. A ditch filled with water, called a **moat**, could be crossed by lowering the drawbridge. The family lived in the tall tower, called a **keep.**

Use the scale beside the picture to see how far thirty meters is on the map. Then estimate, or guess, the distance for each sentence below. Write your estimates on the lines.

1. The height of each tower by the drawbridge is _____ meters.

2. The length of the drawbridge is _____ meters.

3. The height of the keep is _____ meters.

4. The length of the stable building is _____ meters.

5. The distance from the main gate to the keep is _____ meters.

Critical Thinking 3, SV 6214-8

Name _____   Date _____

# Anticipating Probabilities

Circle the word that tells how the person in each story probably feels.

1. The puppy tore open the new pillows. Beth was _____ .

   angry   happy   excited

2. Rosa needed to spell one more word correctly to win the spelling contest. She did not know the word. Rosa was _____ .

   delighted   upset   pleased

3. John was worried because he had missed so much school. His mother watched as he opened his report card. He had gotten very good grades. His mother felt _____ .

   troubled   proud   ashamed

4. Jose was in the school play. He did not know his part very well. It was time for him to go on stage. Jose was _____ .

   angry   glad   frightened

5. Nancy had hoped to go to camp. When the day came for her to leave home, Nancy was sick with the flu. Nancy was _____ .

   surprised   thrilled   sad

6. Jay entered his turtle in a race. Near the end of the race, his turtle moved ahead of the rest. Jay was _____ .

   pleased   bored   disappointed

7. Laura was in a rush getting ready for school. When she got there and found she had on two different colored socks, she was _____ .

   excited   embarrassed   tired

8. Chan did not expect a party on his birthday. When he got home from school and found several of his friends there, he was _____ .

   scared   angry   surprised

Anticipating Probabilities

A. If things usually happen a certain way, we say they will probably happen that way. If, for instance, the river in this picture usually floods in the spring, we could say that it will **probably** flood next spring, too. Decide whether each of the events below usually happens. Then put **X** before those that are probably true.

_____ 1. It will rain tomorrow.

_____ 2. If it rains, the sidewalks will be wet.

_____ 3. The stores will be more crowded in December than in January.

_____ 4. Our school will serve lunch, as it always has done.

_____ 5. We will have the same teacher ten years from now.

_____ 6. More people will take vacations in August than in October.

_____ 7. It will rain sometime in the next month or so.

B. In the space below, rewrite the sentences you did not mark. Change them so they will probably be true.

_____

_____

_____

_____

Inferring

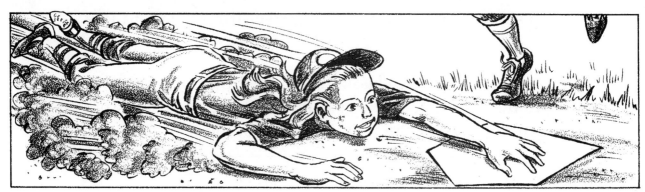

Circle the letter of the best answer for each activity below.

1. The girl looked happy as she crossed home plate.
   a. She was the best player on the team.
   b. She scored the winning run.
   c. She liked baseball.

2. The astronaut wore a heavy space suit.
   a. The suit made it easier to walk on the moon.
   b. The suit was comfortable to wear on Earth.
   c. The astronaut could run easily in the suit on Earth.

3. They dressed themselves. Then they fixed something to eat.
   a. They fixed lunch.
   b. They fixed dinner.
   c. They fixed breakfast.

4. Fred did not want to be alone after he read the book.
   a. He read a funny story.
   b. He read a very sad story.
   c. He read a mystery.

5. Jane ran faster and faster. She broke the tape.
   a. She won the race.
   b. She finished last.
   c. She was not supposed to break the tape.

Name _____ Date _____

Inferring

Read each story. Then write the best answer from the word box for the story.

1. John was sitting with his classmates in the front row. They were listening to the principal. She was calling out the names of students who had won awards during the year. John was in the

playground	auditorium	office	_____.

2. Sue and Percy were watching their favorite team on television. The score was tied in the bottom of the ninth inning. Then the team's best hitter came to bat. Sue and Percy were watching

football	basketball	baseball	_____.

3. Mei was looking forward to visiting her grandmother. They were going to see the baby chicks and ducklings and then go for a ride on the new tractor. Mei's grandmother lived

in an apartment	on a farm	on the beach	_____.

4. From his house, Rudy could see rocky cliffs and snow-capped peaks. He likes to look down at the valley far below him. Rudy lives

on an island	in a city	in the mountains	_____.

5. Mrs. Reed listened to the radio before she went to work. On this day she wore a jacket but put her umbrella in her briefcase. The weather forecast on the radio called for

rain	snow	sunny skies	_____.

Critical Thinking 3, SV 6214-8

Name _____ Date _____

Changes in Word Meanings

A. Sometimes a word has two or more meanings. Study the words and their pictured meanings. Read each sentence below. Think about the underlined word. Write A or B to show which meaning the word has.

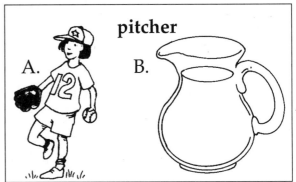

1. _____ She filled the pitcher with lemonade.

2. _____ The pitcher threw the ball to first base.

3. _____ The spaceship will launch in thirty minutes.

4. _____ The tiny launch pulled up to the dock.

B. Each underlined word has several meanings. Read each sentence. Then write a sentence in which the word has a different meaning.

1. The woodpecker clung to the bark of the tree.

   _____

2. The chef poured the cake batter into the pan.

   _____

3. The rider will duck to avoid that low branch.

   _____

4. The sailor opened the hatch of the submarine.

   _____

Changes in Word Meanings

Sometimes people use colorful "sayings" in their speech. Often, the words in a saying do not mean what they usually do. Instead, the words in a "saying" go together to mean something quite different from what the individual words mean. Underline the correct meanings of each "saying" below.

1. If you say, "It's raining cats and dogs," you do not mean that cats and dogs are falling from the sky. What do you mean?
   A. It is raining very hard.
   B. The drops of rain are very big.
   C. It is not raining very hard.

2. What do you think is really meant by, "She is as cool as a cucumber"?
   A. She is like a green vegetable.
   B. She does not let things bother her.
   C. Cucumbers are chilly.

3. "A drop in the bucket" does not mean that there is a drop of something in a bucket. What does it mean?
   A. A small amount of something.
   B. There is water in the bucket.
   C. Only a bucket could hold a drop of water.

4. "Tickled pink" does not mean that someone turned colors. What does it mean?
   A. Someone is delighted.
   B. Someone is laughing a lot.
   C. Someone is being tickled too much.

5. If you say that someone is "in the doghouse," you do not mean he or she is acting like a dog. What do you mean?
   A. Someone is in a small place.
   B. Someone is in trouble.
   C. Someone is acting strangely.

Unit 3
Assessment Test

A. **Changes in Word Meanings**

Change the meanings of the words below by making another drawing.

1. I have the **ring!**   2. I want to be   3. Today is a **fair** day.
                               a **conductor**.

      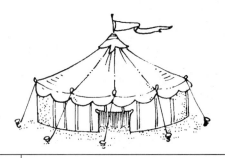

B. **Changes in Word Meanings**
   Inferring

The sentences give clues to the meanings of the underlined words. Write what you think each underlined word means.

1. I will give you a <u>ring</u> when I get home from
   school. If you don't hear from me, please call.   _____

2. At lunchtime there is usually a long <u>line</u>
   at the delicatessen.   _____

3. I can't find my other <u>sock</u> and shoe.   _____

4. The teacher calls the <u>roll</u> at the beginning
   of each school day.   _____

Critical Thinking 3, SV 6214-8   **49**

Name _____ Date _____

C. Ordering Objects

Look at the picture of the circus parade. Then complete 1 and 2.

1. Write the names of the animals from the shortest animal to the tallest animal.

   _____

2. Write the names of the animals in alphabetical order.

   _____

D. Anticipating Probabilities

Look again at the picture. Then write what will probably happen next.

1. The monkey will _____

   _____ .

2. The giraffe will _____

   _____ .

3. The elephant will _____

   _____ .

Name _____ **Date** _____

Unit 4 Analysis

Judging Completeness

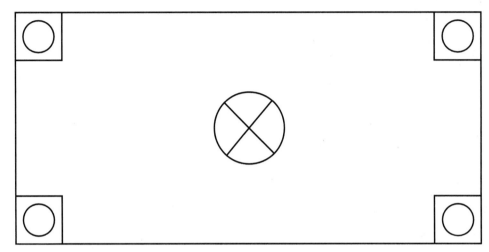

Choose inches or centimeters as your unit of measurement. Then check the two sets of directions below. Which set do you think is better? Explain your choice on the lines below.

A. 1. Draw a rectangle 5 units by 2 1/2 units.
   2. Find the center of the box and draw a circle.
   3. Put an X in the center of the circle. Make the X big enough to touch the sides.
   4. Make a 1/2 square in each corner of the rectangle.
   5. Put a small circle in each corner box. Do not make it touch the sides.

B. 1. Draw a rectangle.
   2. Put a circle in the middle of the box.
   3. Draw an X in the center of the circle.
   4. Make a box out of each corner.
   5. Put a circle in each of the boxes.

_____

_____

_____

_____

Judging Completeness

Read each numbered sentence. Find a sentence with a letter before it that tells the same thing. Write **X** on the line before that sentence.

1. The horses at the farm like to eat hay.

   _____ a. Farm animals eat many things.

   _____ b. Hay is what all farm animals eat.

   _____ c. Hay is what the horses on the farm eat.

2. Ellen wished that her wagon could go faster.

   _____ a. Ellen's wagon was too fast.

   _____ b. Ellen's wagon needed to go faster.

   _____ c. Ellen wished the wagon was not so slow.

3. Patty can read a story very well.

   _____ a. Patty is a good reader.

   _____ b. Patty likes to read.

   _____ c. Patty reads all the time.

4. Juan finished his glass of juice.

   _____ a. Juan likes juice.

   _____ b. Juan put down the juice glass.

   _____ c. Juan drank the juice.

                                      Critical Thinking 3, SV 6214-8

Name _____ Date _____

Relevance of Information

For each activity, put **X** before the **two** things you think are most important.

1. If you wash dishes, you need to know

    _____ where the water heater is.

    _____ where to put the clean dishes.

    _____ where to find the soap.

2. To paint a picture, you need to know

    _____ who painted the last picture.

    _____ where the paint is kept.

    _____ which paper and brush to use.

3. To play in a ball game, you need to know

    _____ where the game will be played.

    _____ where you can get a ball and a bat.

    _____ what the score will be.

4. To use a library, you must know

    _____ how many books are there.

    _____ when the library is open.

    _____ how to get to the library.

Relevance of Information

A. Read each sentence below. Pick a
   word from the list that completes
   the sentence best. Write the word
   in the sentence. Then write the
   word on the correctly numbered
   line in the **Word Box**.

Word Box

1					
2					
3					
4					
5					
6					

stores	better	crowds	police
houses	lights	best	building

1. In cities large _____ of people fill the streets.

2. There are many bright _____ in cities.

3. Some people think cities are _____ places to live than
   the suburbs.

4. Cities have large _____ and fire departments.

5. You may go shopping in many _____ .

6. There are many kinds of _____ to live in.

B. What word now appears in the darker squares of the **Word Box**?

   _____ Can you add anything about cities to the story?

   Write your own city story on another piece of paper.

Abstract or Concrete

Words may tell about **concrete** things or **abstract** things. You can see, hear, touch, taste, or smell a concrete thing, such as a dog. You cannot see, hear, touch, taste, or smell an abstract thing, such as an idea. You can also easily draw a picture of a concrete thing. An abstract thing, like an idea, cannot always be pictured so clearly.

A. Put a check before each concrete thing below.

_____ house   _____ love   _____ price   _____ baby

_____ thought   _____ camel   _____ honor   _____ pencil

_____ screen   _____ courage   _____ shirt   _____ plants

B. Read the sentences. Then circle the underlined words that are abstract.
1. The small child had a <u>fear</u> of the dark.
2. We will use paper <u>plates</u> for the picnic.
3. The lovely <u>flower</u> also smells sweet.
4. Paul showed <u>anger</u> when his sister broke his watch.
5. I have a <u>notion</u> to take a walk.
6. Marcia said she had a strange <u>feeling</u>.
7. Dad's new <u>tie</u> is red, white, and blue.
8. Most parents want <u>happiness</u> for their children.

C. Write a sentence using one of the words that you circled.

_____

_____

- - - Abstract or Concrete - - -

I. Some of the words below name things that people can make. Write **1** before them. Other words name parts of nature. You can see or hear or feel them. Write **2** before them. Still others name things that have to do with ideas or thinking. Write **3** before them.

_____ shoe	_____ flower	_____ love	_____ fog
_____ rain	_____ thunder	_____ ice cube	_____ popcorn
_____ table	_____ wind	_____ lamp	_____ stars
_____ idea	_____ box	_____ imagination	_____ dream

II. In box 1, write all the words you marked **1**. In box 2, write all the words you marked **2**. Then on the line before each word, write which letter fits that word. Write:

A—if you can see the thing named   **C**—if you can feel it
B—if you can hear the thing named   **D**—if you can smell it
       E—if you can taste it

Some will have several letters. If a word you marked **3** fits one of the letters, think about the word again. You might want to make it **1** or **2**.

1		2	
letters	words	letters	words
_____	_____	_____	_____
_____	_____	_____	_____
_____	_____	_____	_____
_____	_____	_____	_____
_____	_____	_____	_____
_____	_____	_____	_____

Critical Thinking 3, SV 6214-8

Logic of Actions

A. Where would you do each of the things listed below? For example, where would you use rhyming words? Read the groups of words under **Where**? You might use rhyming words **in a play** or **in a poem**. Put **1** on the lines before **in a play** and **in a poem**. Match each of the eight numbers to a place. You may match some numbers to more than one place.

1. use rhyming words   5. play running games

2. bounce balls   6. write numbers

3. eat   7. paint pictures

4. fly a plane   8. wear a costume

Where?

_____ a. in math class   _____ f. in the lunchroom

_____ b. in a play   _____ g. on an envelope

_____ c. in art class   _____ h. to a faraway place

_____ d. at a party   _____ i. in a poem

_____ e. in the gym   _____ j. on the playground

B. Write a sentence of your own to tell where you might do each of the following.

1. Tell about places where you could read. _____

_____

2. Tell about places where you could ride in a sled. _____

_____

3. Tell about places where you could sleep. _____

_____

Name _____ Date _____

Logic of Actions

A. Read each sentence and question. Check the parts that make sense.

1. Your best friend is sick. When you visit your friend, which of these things would you take for your friend to use?

_____ books   _____ crayons

_____ tennis racket   _____ bicycle

_____ fishing pole   _____ radio

2. It is raining outside, and your new friend is coming to your house to play. What could you do?

_____ play kickball   _____ play checkers

_____ make model cars   _____ play baseball

_____ play cards   _____ go for a bike ride

3. Your baby brother is always getting into your things in your room. What could you do?

_____ close the door to your room   _____ throw your things away

_____ have your dog guard your door   _____ get another room

_____ place your things out of his reach   _____ play with your brother's toys

B. Imagine that you forgot your lunch money for school. Write three things you could do.

1. _____

2. _____

3. _____

                     Critical Thinking 3, SV 6214-8

Name _____   Date _____

Elements of a Selection

A story is made up of different parts. One very important part is called the **setting**. The setting tells where the story takes place. Look at the settings under each question. Circle the setting that goes with the other information given about the story.

1. Pretend that you want to write a story about the adventures of an alley cat. What would be a likely setting?

    a large city   a small farm   the city zoo

2. You are going to read a story about the life of a sailor. Where would you expect the story to take place?

    on a desert   in a swimming pool   in a boat

3. You are going to write a scary Halloween story. Which of the following places would be the best setting for the story?

    a barnyard   a haunted house   a fire station   your house

4. Imagine that you are writing an adventure story about a group of children. Which setting would you choose?

    a cave   a park   a barn   a beach

5. What would be a good setting for a story about a surprise birthday party?

    someone's basement   the yard   a boat

Critical Thinking 3, SV 6214-8

Name _____ Date _____

Elements of a Selection

Read the story and answer the questions that follow.

When Lola visited her aunt and uncle's farm, her favorite friend was a soft, furry little animal. Its mother would not feed it, so Lola fed it milk from a bottle.

One day the little creature strayed away from the rest of the flock. Lola searched for it for a long time. It finally made a tiny bleat, and Lola heard it. She was able to lead it home by holding out the bottle of milk.

1. Where does the story take place?

_____

2. What kind of animal was Lola's favorite friend?

_____

3. Write a good title for this story.

_____

4. How would Lola's part in the story change if the animal were a tiger?

_____

5. How would the story change if Lola had not heard the tiny bleat?

_____

6. How would the story change if Lola's aunt and uncle told her not to go near the animals?

_____

Critical Thinking 3, SV 6214-8

Story Logic

Number each story to show the correct story order. Put **1** before the first part. Put **2** before the middle part. Put **3** before the last part.

_____ Maria's older brother Juan worked with animals at the natural science center. Maria went to a pay phone and asked Juan to come right away to free the sea gull.

_____ She followed the sound to a big ball of wire. A sea gull was tangled in the wire. Maria tried to get close to the gull, but it only became more tangled.

_____ Maria was walking along the beach. Suddenly, she heard a loud cry.

_____ Amy was surprised when her mother's best friend drove by! She and Amy put the bike into the trunk of the car. Later, Amy and her cousin fixed the tire.

_____ Amy wanted to visit her cousin. Mother said that Amy could go on her bicycle.

_____ Amy had a flat tire on the way. She started pushing the bicycle along.

_____ He was in luck! The fish were really biting today. He caught so many fish that he could not carry them home.

_____ He kept six fish and gave the rest to other people at the beach.

_____ Jesse walked down to the beach with his fishing pole and bait. He hoped to catch a few fish for dinner.

Story Logic

Each story below has a sentence or a group of words that does not belong. Underline the group of words that you would take out of each story.

1. Yesterday our class went on a picnic to the park. Everyone brought sack lunches. Jack does not like picnics. We sat under the trees and ate lunch. It was a nice day for a picnic.

2. A raccoon sometimes makes its home in a tree trunk. There are many kinds of trees, too. It sleeps in the tree trunk all day and hunts at night for mice and insects.

3. Students keep busy at school. They read, write, do math, and play. The library is on the first floor. They do many different things each day.

4. There are several things you should know about sentences. Sentences begin with a capital letter. They end with a period or other punctuation mark. Sentences also have a subject and a predicate. Some sentences are silly.

5. Helen and Rita stayed after school today to help the teacher. They cleaned erasers, washed the boards, and looked out the window. They might help again tomorrow.

6. Children wear warm clothes to play in the snow. They put on mittens and boots. They make snowballs and slide down hills on sleds. It is hard to drive on a snowy road.

7. Some people are tall and others are short. Some people look sad and others look happy. My dog looks sad. No two people are alike.

8. The work on a flower garden may begin in the fall. That's when bulbs are planted. In early spring the green plants peek through the ground. Robins begin to sing. Soon, tulips, daffodils, and irises are blooming in the garden.

Name _____ Date _____

Recognizing Fallacies

Each sentence below gives only two choices. If only two choices are possible, write **T** for true before the sentence. If you can think of more choices than the sentence gives you, put **F** for false.

Examples:	**F**	You are either at school or at home. (You might be at a store or another place.)
	T	Either you have freckles or you don't.

_____ 1. Fleas jump only onto dogs or cats.

_____ 2. Either you are alive, or you are not alive.

_____ 3. You are either hungry or full.

_____ 4. You are either playing or working.

_____ 5. You may either leave or stay here.

_____ 6. Vegetables are either green or yellow.

_____ 7. Either you tell the truth, or you tell lies.

_____ 8. Either you are moving, or you are staying still.

_____ 9. A glass is either empty or full.

_____ 10. The fan is either on or off.

_____ 11. Either you wear glasses, or you do not wear glasses.

_____ 12. You write with either your left hand or your right hand.

_____ 13. Your hair is either blonde or brown.

_____ 14. Your parent is either a mother or a father.

Name _____ Date _____

Recognizing Fallacies

Sometimes if you are near the wrong thing or with a person who did something wrong, you may get into trouble. Put **X** before the sentences below which tell about places or happenings that could get you into trouble.

_____ 1. You are grocery shopping with your parents.

_____ 2. Your friend puts some comic books in your desk. You are not supposed to have them at school.

_____ 3. You are at the ballpark with your father and mother.

_____ 4. You and your friend find some rings. Later, you find out they were stolen.

_____ 5. You are at the circus with your uncle.

_____ 6. You are riding your bicycle where your parents said you could.

_____ 7. You did your school work all by yourself. But you have all the same wrong answers as your best friend.

_____ 8. You found a dime on the sidewalk.

_____ 9. You took some fruit from the refrigerator. Later, the refrigerator door was found standing open.

_____ 10. You are going outside to play.

_____ 11. You are standing next to a broken window.

_____ 12. You washed your bicycle. Later, your parents found that water was still pouring from the hose.

_____ 13. You often play with a group of children who have been seen breaking street lights.

_____ 14. There is broken glass in the kitchen, and you have been the only one at home today.

Critical Thinking 3, SV 6214-8

Unit 4
Assessment Test

A. Judging Completeness

Look at the picture of an antique store window. Some of the items in the window have missing parts. In the sentences below, circle the word that tells what is needed to complete each item.

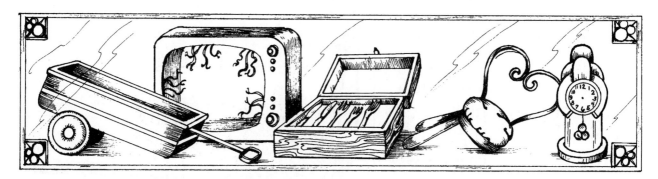

1. The clock needs   legs   hands   eyes.

2. The wagon needs   wheels   windows   doors.

3. The television needs a   handle   screen   frame.

4. The silverware chest is missing   forks   spoons   knives.

5. The chair needs   legs   wheels   sheets.

B. Relevance of Information

Pretend that the items pictured above are complete. Write the name of the item you would use for each task.

1. to set the table for dinner _____

2. to sit at a desk to do homework _____

3. to take home many bags of groceries _____

4. to get to school on time _____

5. to get the latest news report _____

Critical Thinking 3, SV 6214-8   **65**

Assessment Test (p. 2)

C. Abstract or Concrete

Helena is going to spend the night at her friend Kay's house. Help Helena by writing on the lines in the duffel bag the things that she can pack.

pajamas	bathrobe
excitement	laughter
dreams	friendship
book	toothbrush
sleep	fun
comb	slippers
brush	eagerness

D. Story Logic

Read the sentences below to see if they make sense. The last sentence must make sense based on the information given in the first two sentences. Copy the last sentence if it makes sense.

1. Helena often spends the night at Kay's house. Kay sometimes spends the night at Helena's house. Helena and Kay are friends.

_____

2. Dogs make good pets. Sam has a dog. Sam's dog is a good pet.

_____

3. Many trees have fruit. The birch is a tree. The elm has fruit.

_____

Name _____   Date _____

Unit 5 Synthesis
Communicating Ideas

The International Morse Code is a famous way to send messages. It uses dots, dashes, and spaces. Can you read the coded message at the bottom? Look at the chart to find each symbol and the letter it stands for. Write each letter in a box under the symbol to make a sentence.

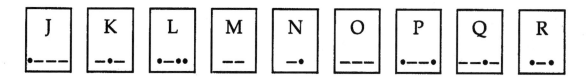

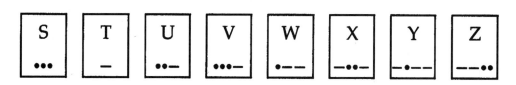

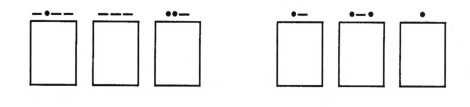

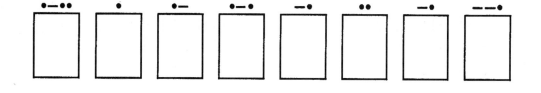

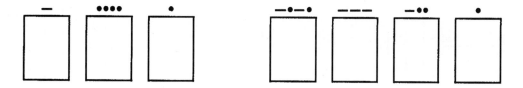

    Critical Thinking 3, SV 6214-8

Communicating Ideas

Some children in the class measured how tall they are:

Cindy is 44 inches tall.

Celia is 38 inches tall.

Marco is 42 inches tall.

Sally is 36 inches tall.

Jiro is 46 inches tall.

Rex is 48 inches tall.

Look at the graph below. Rex is the tallest child, so his name is written at the top. See that a line has been drawn to show his height on the graph. Write the name of the second tallest child on the second blank and draw a line to show the height. Go on until all the children's heights are shown.

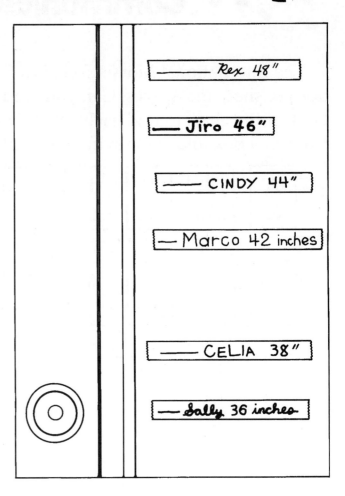

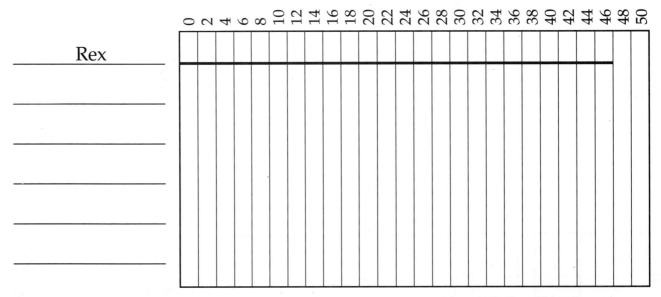

inches

Rex

Communicating Ideas

A. Signs communicate messages to drivers. Write the letter of each sign next to its message.

1. _____ No bicycles are allowed on this road.

2. _____ No U-turns are allowed here.

3. _____ This is a place where people cross the street.

4. _____ No right turn is allowed here.

5. _____ Warning! This is a railroad crossing.

6. _____ Warning! Deer cross the road here.

B. Think of two messages you could communicate using signs. Draw your signs below. Next to each sign, explain what it means and where you would put it.

 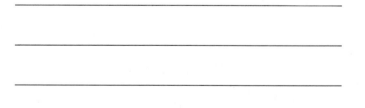

Planning Projects

A. Pretend that the art teacher has asked your class to make valentines. Underline any of the following things you could use.

tacks	scissors	paste	music
lace	crayons	ruler	white paper
red paper	clock	book	yarn

B. How should the valentines be made? Check the way you think is best.

_____ Each person should work alone.

_____ Two or three students should work together.

_____ The class should make one big valentine.

C. How much time should be used? Check your choice.

_____ Just one art period should be used.

_____ More than one art period should be used.

_____ An art period and some time at recess should be used.

_____ Whatever time is needed to get the job done should be used.

D. Do you think each of the three problems considered above is important?

_____ Why or why not? _____

_____

E. What else would you like to know about valentine making?

_____

_____

_____

Planning Projects

A. Nat was working on a wildlife display. He planned to make a plaster cast of some animal tracks he had seen. Check the things below that Nat might do.

_____ 1. call a friend on the telephone

_____ 2. talk to an adult about how to make a cast

_____ 3. feed his dog

_____ 4. collect materials

_____ 5. find out what the animal is

_____ 6. pour water on the tracks

B. These are the steps that Nat has to follow to make the plaster cast. 1 is next to the first thing that Nat should do. Number the rest of the steps in the order he should follow.

_____ Let the plaster get hard.

_____ Read and follow the directions to mix the plaster of paris.

_____ Pour the plaster of paris into the cardboard mold.

__1__ Place a ring of cardboard around the track to make a mold.

_____ Remove the cardboard mold when the plaster is hard.

_____ Turn the plaster cast over to see the raised animal track on the other side.

C. Once Nat has made his cast, he still needs to do some other things before his wildlife display is ready. Write at least two more things that you think Nat should do.

1. _____

2. _____

Name _____   Date _____

Building Hypotheses

Study the picture. Then answer the questions.

1. What has happened in the picture?

_____

_____

2. Why has this happened?

_____

_____

3. What do you think will happen next?

_____

_____

Critical Thinking 3, SV 6214-8

Building Hypotheses

A. Read the story. Then check the sentence that gives the most likely reason for what happened.

Tim likes to cook. One day he made potato salad. As a dressing, he mixed sour cream and a little salt. Tim's family liked the salad. A few days later Tim made potato salad again. This time he used mayonnaise and salt as the dressing. Tim's family said the salad was too salty. The next time that Tim made potato salad dressing, he used yogurt and salt. Everyone said the dressing was fine.

Why was the second salad unsuccessful?

_____ People have different tastes.

_____ Tim's family doesn't like salt.

_____ Mayonnaise already has salt in it.

_____ The third salad was better.

B. How do you think Tim could make a salad dressing with mayonnaise that his family will like?

_____

_____

Building Hypotheses

Read the story. Then write the clues that the detective used to solve the mystery.

The Muffin Mystery

Someone ate the muffins that Mr. Selby left on the kitchen table. "They were right out of the oven," Mr. Selby told Detective Frank. "I left them here to cool."

"Hmmm," said Detective Frank as he looked around. "Whoever ate the muffins must be able to reach the table. Also, the thief did not eat all of the muffins, just little pecks from each one."

Detective Frank questioned the cat, the parrot, and the dog. These were the answers they gave.

"I don't like muffins," purred the cat.

Brushing a crumb from its feathers, the parrot said, "I don't know what you're talking about. But would you be kind enough to give me a nice cold drink of water? My mouth hurts."

"I do like muffins," said the dog. "But I can't reach the table top."

Detective Frank gave the parrot some water.

"Well, who ate my muffins?" asked Mr. Selby.

"It was this naughty parrot, I'm afraid!" answered Detective Frank.

Write 4 clues that helped Detective Frank.

_____

_____

_____

_____

 Critical Thinking 3, SV 6214-8

Drawing Conclusions

monkey

turtle

pig

dog

kitten

mouse

The children in Cindy's class are having a pet parade. They want to give prizes to the different animals. You are the judge.

1. Which animal would you choose as the most unusual?

_____ Why? _____

2. Which animal would you choose as the easiest to care for?

_____ Why? _____

3. Which animal would you choose as the most helpful to its owner?

_____ Why? _____

4. Which animal would you choose as the best at learning things?

_____ Why? _____

Drawing Conclusions

Read each story. Then check the sentence under it that gives the best conclusion.

1.   It was a crisp fall day. Mr. Larch drove slowly so nothing would fall off his truck. Anyway, he had to stop often to make pickups. At each stop Mr. Larch put on his gloves, got out, and threw big bags onto his truck. Almost all the leaves were off the trees and off the lawns, Mr. Larch noted. It would be a busy day.

_____   Mr. Larch is picking up people's laundry.

_____   Mr. Larch is collecting bags of leaves.

_____   Mr. Larch is gathering sacks of mail.

2.   Steve washed his finger in the sink. Then he found a bandage and put it on. Holding his finger carefully, Steve went back to his desk, took out a new sheet of paper, and began to write.

_____   Steve cut his finger on a piece of paper.

_____   Steve cut his finger on the sink.

_____   Steve cut his finger on his desk.

3.   Marie looked around the airport helplessly. She asked some people for directions but could not really understand what they said. Marie saw a sign, but she wasn't sure what it meant, either. Finally, Marie took a small book out of her bag and hunted through it.

_____   Marie was a child who had lost her mother in an airport.

_____   The airport was too noisy for Marie to understand anything.

_____   Marie was in a foreign country and did not speak the language there.

Proposing Alternatives

Sometimes old or worn-out things can be used in new ways. Write the name of the old item under the new way to use it. See if you can think of some more uses for these old things.

a car that won't run   newspapers   old shoes
empty plastic bottles   torn shirts   old greeting cards

New Ways to Use Old Things

1. You could use the parts to make a scooter.

   _____

2. You could use them to store liquids.

   _____

3. You could make papier-mâché out of them.

   _____

4. You could cut out the decorations and make new ones of your own.

   _____

5. You could dust the furniture with them.

   _____

6. You could use the tongue for a bookmark.

   _____

Critical Thinking 3, SV 6214-8

⟋--- Proposing Alternatives ---⟍

Here are some common things that could be used in many different ways. Put on your thinking cap. Write as many different uses for each thing as you can. Remember, you can do anything you want to with the objects. For example, you could cut or paste or fold them.

1.

ball of yarn

_____

_____

_____

2.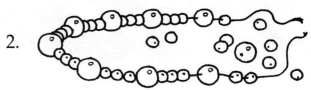

broken necklace

_____

_____

_____

3.

cardboard tubes

_____

_____

_____

4.

clothespins

_____

_____

_____

5.

plastic tubing

_____

_____

_____

6.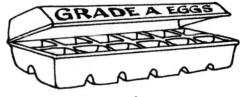

egg carton

_____

_____

_____

Critical Thinking 3, SV 6214-8

Unit 5

Assessment Test

A. Communicating Ideas

The Mayans lived many hundreds of years ago. The symbol on the right is a number from their writing system. Each bar stands for **5**. Each dot stands for **1**. So this symbol means **12**. The chart below should show symbols for the numbers **1** to **20**. Use Mayan symbols to fill in the missing numbers.

•	• •		• • • •
___		• • ___	
		• ___	
• • • ═══	• • • • ═══		• ═══
		• • • • ═══	

B. Planning Projects

Next to each activity on the left, write the letters of the things you need to do that activity.

_____ 1. write in code   a. needle   e. thread

_____ 2. wash your hands   b. soap   f. recipe

_____ 3. sew a seam   c. paper   g. water

_____ 4. make bread   d. pencil   h. flour

Assessment Test (p. 2)

C. Developing Conclusions

At the Souvenir Shop, only one salesperson is waiting on customers. Where is that person? Read each clue. Find the department mentioned. Put an **X** on it on the map. Which one is left? You've solved the mystery!

1. The salesperson in Jewelry is out sick.

2. The salesperson in T-Shirts is on the phone.

3. The clerks in Hats and Hankies are having a meeting.

4. Everyone in Posters and Maps is taking a break.

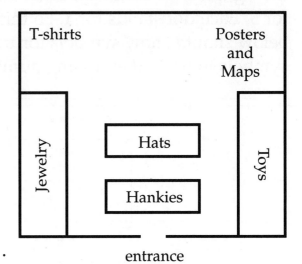

The salesperson is in _____ .

D. Proposing Alternatives

For each item, write another use.

1. map   hang it on a wall

   _____

2. bicycle   ride it to school

   _____

3. computer   play a game

   _____

4. trunk   pack clothes

   _____

                                     Critical Thinking 3, SV 6214-8

Name _____ Date _____

Unit 6 Evaluation
Testing Generalizations

Read each statement and the words below it. If the statement is true for all of the words, write **yes** on the line. If the statement is not true for some words, write **no** on the line. Put **X** on the words that make the statement wrong.

_____ 1. The pairs of words are opposites.
dark—light   yes—no   big—large

_____ 2. All of these words rhyme.
bark   mark   park   lack   dark

_____ 3. Each word has three syllables.
family   bicycle   animal   tomorrow

_____ 4. The words in each pair sound the same.
buy—bye   bear—bare   too—two   through—threw

_____ 5. All of the words end with the same two consonants.
pink   rink   sing   think   sink

_____ 6. The words in each pair mean about the same.
noisy—loud   circle—ring   touch—feel

_____ 7. These words have three letters that are the same.
dear   heart   wear   beard   earth

_____ 8. These words have the same vowel sound.
load   pole   know   toe   bone

_____ 9. Since these words end in **s**, they are all plurals.
dogs   rugs   this   bus   lips

_____ 10. These words have the same vowel sound.
torn   born   morn   rock   worn

_____ 11. These words are in alphabetical order.
stamp   twin   work   your   zone

Testing Generalizations

Each of these sentences states something that is not always true. Write a sentence to prove that the statement is not always true.

Example: In a city, everyone lives in an apartment building.
Esmerita lives in a house.

1. People who work always go to an office.

   _____

2. All doctors wear eyeglasses.

   _____

3. Everyone who goes to the beach knows how to swim.

   _____

4. All cats are pets.

   _____

5. Outdoor games are always played with a ball.

   _____

6. All teachers are women.

   _____

7. Everyone who goes to school rides a bus.

   _____

8. All boats have motors.

   _____

Developing Criteria

kitten

fish

parakeet

dog

pony

A. Answer these questions about the pets above.

1. Which is the most quiet? _____

2. Which one can guard your house? _____

3. Which one can chirp merrily? _____

4. Which could you **not** play with? _____

5. Which would you **not** keep in your house? _____

6. Which is the easiest to take on a trip? _____

B. What things do you think are most important to keep in mind in choosing a pet?

_____

_____

Developing Criteria

A. Imagine that you are buying books for each of the people described below. Use what you read about each person to choose the books he or she would enjoy most. Write the letters of the best book choices before each name.

a.    b.    c.    d.

e.    f.    g.

1. _____ Alex—He is interested in animals. He enjoys working at his mom's pet store. He has a big aquarium at home. He likes to read about real and imaginary animals.

2. _____ Sara—She loves science. She likes to build things, try to figure out how things work, and solve all kinds of mysteries. She would like to be an inventor when she grows up.

B. What things do you keep in mind when you choose a book for

yourself? _____

_____

Decide which book shown above you might enjoy. Write its title and give two reasons for your choice.

_____

_____

Critical Thinking 3, SV 6214-8

Judging Accuracy

When you read or listen, ask yourself if what is written or said makes sense. Sometimes people say one thing and then another that is different. When this happens, it is hard to know what they really mean.

Read these paragraphs. Find two sentences in each that **contradict**, or say the opposite thing. Underline those sentences.

1. Elisha Otis invented the elevator in 1852. With his invention people could go from floor to floor in a building without climbing stairs. This invention made it possible for people to build tall skyscrapers. Thank you, Mr. Otis, for inventing the escalator.

2. Pioneers worked hard from morning to night. They hunted, plowed the land, and made their own clothes. They usually sat around and played games. They also made their own tools, built their homes, and wove their own cloth.

3. Many people remember Ben Franklin because he did an experiment with a kite and lightning. Ben Franklin is known for many other things, too. He started a hospital, a college, and a library. He also ran a print shop. Ben Franklin never did any scientific work, however.

4. The way a clown's face is painted is very important. Each clown's face is different from all the other clowns. When you go to the circus, all the clowns look alike.

5. Schools in India are not like schools here. Many boys and girls in India do not go to school. Instead of going to school, they stay at home and help with the work. Children in India who do not go to school get to play all day.

6. The Wright brothers were interested in flying. They read books about flying and drew pictures of things that might fly. They thought flying was boring. In 1900 they built a glider and tried to fly it.

Judging Accuracy

When you write a report, you get information from different places or sources. It is important to make good choices about the sources that you use.

Read the paragraph below. Then fill in each blank with one of the sources given in the box. Choose the best source for each sentence.

dictionary	encyclopedia	map	song
chart	poem	radio	girl from Egypt

The _____ shows that Egypt

is in Africa. The capital of Egypt is Cairo. The

_____ says that it is pronounced kī´rō.

I read in the _____ that most people in

Egypt are farmers. Just this morning on the

_____ there was a report about how

many people live along the Nile. It provides most of the

country's water. I would like to meet a _____

to find out more about life in Egypt.

    Critical Thinking 3, SV 6214-8

Name _____   Date _____

Making Decisions

There are often many ways to do something. Some ways are better than others. It is a good idea to stop and think about all the possibilities before you decide.

Each sentence tells about what someone wants to do. The three sentences that follow give ways it could be done. Underline the sentence that you think tells the best way.

1. Mr. Blake wants to sell his car.
   a. He could put a sign in his apartment window.
   b. He could run an ad in the newspaper.
   c. He could put a note on the bulletin board in the library.

2. Leon wants to win the costume contest.
   a. He could make a costume that no one else has thought of.
   b. He could wear his costume from last year.
   c. He could wear the costume he wore in the school play.

3. Rita wants to get extra sleep so she will have more energy for playing soccer.
   a. She could sleep later in the morning.
   b. She could take naps after school.
   c. She could go to bed earlier at night.

4. Honey wants to surprise her Dad with a great birthday gift.
   a. She could ask him what he wants.
   b. She could watch and listen to find out what he might need or like.
   c. She could ask the clerk in the store for help.

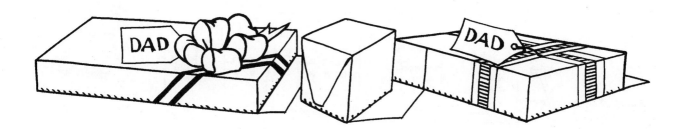

Name _____   Date _____

Making Decisions

When you decide to do something, you want to do it correctly. Often you can follow rules or guidelines that tell you how something should be done.

Read the guidelines that tell how to make something. Then read the paragraph that Raoul wrote.

- List the materials you need.
- Tell things in order.
- Use time words, such as **first**, **next**, **then**, and **last**.

First, scoop up a large pile of sand with your hands. Next, get pails of water and wet the sand down so you can work with it. Then, begin molding the sand into the shape you want. You may need to add more sand and water as you work. The last thing you do is put the finishing touches on your sculpture. Use a plastic knife or spoon to carve the features.

1. What did Raoul leave out in his directions?

_____

2. Write the part of the directions that Raoul left out.

_____

_____

_____

                    Critical Thinking 3, SV 6214-8

Identifying Values

A. Listed below are some things you can do. Some of them are helpful and fair. Put **H** in front of these. Some of the statements describe unfair acts or acts that would not be helpful. Put **X** in front of those acts.

_____ 1. You could help your parents clean the house.

_____ 2. You could leave your toys all over the room.

_____ 3. You could always fight to be the first batter in the ball game.

_____ 4. You could ask your new neighbor to play with you and your friends.

_____ 5. You could pick up the coat on the floor, even though it is not yours.

_____ 6. You could take a big handful of popcorn when there is not enough for everyone.

B. Choose one of the two ways to finish the sentences below. Circle the ending that tells what you would do.

1. You saw Lois drop some paper in the park. You should

   ignore it.

   put the paper in the trash can.

2. You bought a whistle that does not work. You should

   go back to the store and trade it for another whistle.

   throw it away.

3. You saw Dean push a younger boy down on the playground. You should

   push Dean down.

   try to help the younger boy.

Identifying Values

Read the story. Then write answers to the questions.

Jonathan didn't know what he was going to do. His best friends, Mike and Chris, had just left on vacation for the rest of the summer. The next two months were going to be very lonely!

After a few days, Jonathan started playing with Brian. Brian lived down the block. Jonathan hadn't played with Brian before because Mike and Chris didn't like Brian. As the summer days sped by, the two boys became the best of friends. They did everything together.

Jonathan and Brian were in the middle of an exciting game near the summer's end. The doorbell rang, and there stood Mike and Chris. They rushed in, full of stories about their summer. But they stopped short when they saw Brian. "What's he doing here?" whispered Mike. "Tell him to go home."

1. What are three things Jonathan might do?

   a. _____

   _____

   b. _____

   _____

   c. _____

   _____

2. What do you think Jonathan should do? Why?

   _____

   _____

   _____

                    Critical Thinking 3, SV 6214-8

Name _____ **Date** _____

Mood of a Story

Read the sentences. Try to put yourself in the place of the characters. How do they feel? Circle the word that best describes the feeling.

1. Mom settled back in her chair, gave a happy sigh, and opened her book.
   a. content   b. nervous   c. amused

2. As night fell, the woods seemed to close in on us. Strange noises filled the air, and I was sure that something lurked behind every tree or bush.
   a. pleasant   b. scary   c. calm

3. The young man who had been sick won the prize for his story.
   a. disturbed   b. pleased   c. unhappy

4. The girl who did the high-wire circus act slipped, started falling, and then quickly got back on the wire.
   a. excited   b. worried   c. sad

5. Martin made a new friend when he went to the playground.
   a. glad   b. sorry   c. angry

6. Pete slammed the book down on his desk. His face was red.
   a. happy   b. angry   c. sad

7. The blazing sun burned my skin until it was too sore to touch. I groaned.
   a. proud   b. unhappy   c. pleasant

8. The glowing fire kept us warm while we popped corn and toasted marshmallows. Outside, the snowflakes danced at the windows.
   a. restless   b. lonely   c. cozy

Critical Thinking 3, SV 6214-8

Mood of a Story

Read the paragraph. Then answer the questions.

Amy saw that the big easy chair was empty. She smiled to herself, then went and got her potholder loom and the colored loops that went with it. She turned on the lamp against the late afternoon darkness and found her favorite music station on the radio. Then Amy sank into the comfortable chair with a sigh. Outside the storm raged. The rain beat against the windows, but Amy didn't mind. Her foot tapped to the soft music as she wove a pretty potholder on her loom.

1. In this story, how does Amy feel?

_____

_____

2. How would you describe the place where the story takes place?

_____

_____

_____

3. What is happening outside the place where Amy is?

_____

_____

_____

Unit 6
Assessment Test

A. Testing Generalizations

Read each statement and the words which follow it. If the statement is true, write **true** on the line. If the statement is not true about all the items, write **not true**.

1. _____ These items can all be found in a bedroom.
   bathtub bed chest rug pillow
2. _____ These items can all be read.
   book magazine newspaper letter sign
3. _____ These animals all live in the water.
   shark lobster frog seahorse seal
4. _____ These are different kinds of flowers.
   rose violet tulip banana daisy
5. _____ You can climb all of these things.
   ladder floor stairs rope mountain

B. Developing Criteria

Fill in the chart to find out who is who. Then write the name of each boy under his picture.

Fred	Ned
Ed	Ted

Ned and Ted have dark eyes.
Ed, Ned, and Fred have black hair.
Ted and Fred wear glasses.

Critical Thinking 3, SV 6214-8

Assessment Test (p. 2)

C. Judging Accuracy

Read the two paragraphs. Underline the conclusion in each paragraph. Circle the conclusion that does not make sense.

1. Andy struck out for the third time today. He angrily threw the bat on the ground. Then he picked up his glove and ran off toward home. Andy was a good sport.

2. Meg took Butter, her golden retriever, for his second walk of the day. When they got home she fed him, brushed his coat, and tried again to teach him to stay at her command. Meg is a caring pet owner.

D. Identifying Values

Read the story. Then answer the questions.

Lena was disappointed! She'd saved all summer for new gym shoes. She was sure they'd help her make the basketball team. But today she found that the price had gone up. She needed just fifty cents more!

Lena looked ahead and saw a man picking up change from the sidewalk. The man had dropped it while he was feeding a parking meter. As the man straightened up and began walking away, Lena noticed two quarters the man hadn't picked up.

1. What things might Lena do? _____

_____

_____

2. What do you think Lena should do? Why? _____

_____

_____

Answer Key

Page 6 - A. 1. hands 2. wheels 3. screen 4. spoons 5. legs **B.** 1. silverware chest 2. chair 3. wagon 4. clock 5. television

Page 7 - C. 3 dots, line with 1 dot, line with 3 dots, line with 4 dots, 2 lines, 2 lines with 2 dots, 3 lines, 3 lines with 2 dots, 3 lines with 3 dots, 4 lines **D.** 1. telephone call 2. many customers 3. piece of clothing 4. list of names

Page 9 - 2. relatives 3. clothes 4. furniture 5. tools 6. sports

Page 10 - 1. salmon, shrimp, perch, tuna 2. peaches, cherries, apples, watermelon 3. hot dogs, turkey, beef, chicken 4. corn, broccoli, potatoes, carrots

Page 11 - 1. triangles, three 2. rectangles, four 3. squares, equal 4. circles, Circles have no sides.

Page 12 - A. 1. F 2. R 3. F 4. R 5. F 6. R 7. R 8. R 9. R 10. F 11. F 12. F **B.** 1. R 2. F 3. R 4. R 5. F 6. F **C.** Sentences will vary.

Page 13 - A. 1. X 2. Y 3. X 4. Y 5. Y 6. X 7. Y 8. Y **B.** Sentences will vary.

Page 14 - 1. O 2. F 3. O 4. F 5. O 6. F 7. F 8. F 9. O 10. O 11. F 12. O 13. O 14. F

Page 15 - Sentences will vary.

Page 16 - 1. D 2. E 3. D 4. E 5. D 6. D 7. D 8. E 9. D 10. E

Page 17 - 1. city 2. flower 3. month 4. game 5. tree 6. dessert

Page 18 - sea, plankton, floor, float, animal, crabs, sponges, smaller

Page 19 - Homes: Many names for homes A. Palace B. Mansion C. House D. Cottage **Seeds:** Travel in many ways A. Birds B. Winds C. Insects D. Animals' fur E. Fall from bushes and trees

Page 20 - A. 1. F, R 2. R, F 3. F, R **B. I.** A. Elves B. Unicorn C. Leprechaun **II.** A. Shoemaker B. Eagle C. Miner

Page 21 - C. 1. bedding: pillow, sheet, mattress, blanket, quilt 2. dishes: plate, saucer, cup, bowl, platter 3. footwear: shoes, slippers, sandals, boots **D.** Sentences will vary.

Page 22 - 1. swings, seesaw, slide 2. babies, flowers 3. iron, bricks, concrete 4. goats, horses, camels 5. balloon, football, tire 6. milk, water, juice 7. elephant, truck, stove, TV 8. firecracker, horn, drum

Page 23 - A. 1. b. They are all animals. 2. c. They are all used to hold things together. 3. b. They all have printed words in them. 4. b. They all have pits. **B.** Sentences will vary.

Page 24 - heading, signature, inside address, salutation, body, close

Page 25 - A. Last two notes in each line should be circled. **B.** beginning, characters, time, place, things happen, exciting point, problem is solved, ends

Page 26 - A. 1. Washing Dishes 2, 3, 1, 4 **2.** Getting Ready for School 3, 2, 4, 1 **3.** Making a Model Airplane 4, 1, 3, 2 **4.** Baking a Cake 2, 3, 1, 4 **B.** Answers will vary.

Page 27 - Wrapping a Present 2, 3, 4, 5, 1 A Frog's Life 3, 2, 4, 1

Page 28 - 1. Fox River 2. near the library 3. Center Street 4. Valley Road 5. north and south

Page 29 - 5 squares, 6 rectangles, 17 triangles

Page 30 - A. 1. afraid 2. build 3. help 4. under 5. tired Answer to riddle: ruler **B.** 1. arrive 2. seldom 3. small 4. wrong Answer to riddle: a saw

Page 31 - A. 1. weary 2. mosquito 3. crossly 4. rude 5. dodging **B.** 1. imaginary 2. weighty 3. hit 4. annoying 5. entertaining

Page 32 - 1. Main Idea: Honeybees help people. Details: a. Bees make honey. b. Beeswax is used to make useful things. c. Bees fertilize flowers. 2. Main Idea: things to do outside in winter. Details: a. ice-skate on ponds b. sled down hills c. go skiing

Page 33 - 1. Circle: Ants build many kinds of nests. Mark through: Termites also burrow. 2. Circle: Babies cry to tell us something. Mark through: It is fun to play with dolls. 3. Circle: You never know where you'll find a bird nest! Mark through: Other animals live in trees, too. 4. Circle: Watches come in many different styles. Mark through: Today is September 2. 5. Circle: As you can tell, games can be played both indoors and out. Mark through: Bicycling is fun outdoors, too.

Page 34 - 1. Learning About Barges 2. Harbor Helpers 3. Facts About Houseboats

Page 35 - A. 2. C 3. K 4. I 5. J 6. O 7. P 8. T 9. U 10. Y **B.** 1. O I C U 2. B C N U 3. R U O K

Page 36 - 1, 4, 3, 5, 2

Page 37 - A. 1. Washington, D.C., has many places to visit. 2. the Capitol 3. spectacular **B.** beautiful, interesting, historic

Page 38 - C. 1. B 2. A, C 3. B, C, D **D.** Answers will vary.

Page 39 - I. A. 2, 4, 3, 1 **B.** 1, 4, 2, 3 **II. C.** 3, 1, 2, 4 **D.** 3, 1, 2, 4 **III.** Answers will vary.

Page 40 - 1. circle 2. line with 3 dots 3. square with diagonal from bottom left corner to top right corner 4. S 5. square shaded almost full 6. 24 7. one horizontal line 8. L 9. circle with top right quarter shaded 10. 1 + 5

Page 41 - A. 1. sharpen a pencil 2. wash the windows 3. take out the trash 4. go swimming 5. feed the dog 6. eat a cookie **B.** 1. ten 2. half a minute 3. fifteen minutes 4. twenty

Page 42 - 1. 25 2. 15 3. 25 4. 30 5. 75

Page 43 - 1. angry 2. upset 3. proud 4. frightened 5. sad 6. pleased 7. embarrassed 8. surprised

Page 44 - A. 2, 3, 4, 6, 7 **B.** Sentences will vary.

Page 45 - 1. Answers will vary. 2. a 3. c 4. Answers will vary. 5. a

Page 46 - 1. auditorium 2. baseball 3. on a farm 4. in the mountains 5. rain

Page 47 - A. 1. B 2. A 3. A 4. B **B.** Answers will vary.

Page 48 -1. A. It is raining very hard. 2. B. She does not let things bother her. 3. A. A small amount of something. 4. A. Someone is delighted. 5. B. Someone is in trouble.

Page 49 - A. 1. picture of a ring (jewelry) or the phone ringing 2. picure of a train conductor 3. picture of a clear day **B.** 1. telephone call 2. many customers 3. piece of clothing 4. list of names

Page 50 - C. 1. monkeys, lions, horses, elephants, giraffes 2. elephants, giraffes, horses, lions, monkeys **D.** Answers will vary.

Page 51 - Answers may vary, but most pupils will choose A because the directions are more precise and complete.

Page 52 - 1. c 2. c 3. a 4. c

Page 53 - 1. where to put the clean dishes, where to find the soap 2. where the paint is kept, which paper and brush to use 3. where the game will be played, where you can get a ball and a bat 4. when the library is open, how to get to the library

Page 54 - **A.** 1. crowds 2. lights 3. better 4. police 5. stores 6. houses **B.** cities

Page 55 - **A.** house, screen, camel, shirt, baby, pencil, plants **B.** 1. fear 4. anger 5. notion 6. feeling 8. happiness **C.** Sentences will vary.

Page 56 - **I.** 1 shoe, 2 rain, 1 table, 3 idea, 2 flower, 2 thunder, 2 wind , 1 box , 3 love, 1 ice cube, 1 lamp, 3 imagination, 2 fog, 1 popcorn, 2 stars, 3 dream **II. Box 1** A, C, D shoe, A, C table, A, C box, A, C, E ice cube, A, C lamp, A, B, C, D, E popcorn **Box 2** A, B, C, E rain, A, C, D flower, B thunder, B, C wind, A fog, A stars

Page 57 - **A.** a. 6 b. 1,8 c. 7 d. 2,3,5,8 e. 2,5 f. 3 g. 6 h. 4 i. 1 j. 2, 4, 5 **B.** Answers will vary.

Page 58 - **A.** 1. books, crayons, radio 2. make model cars, play cards, play checkers 3. close the door to your room, place your things out of his reach **B.** Responses will vary.

Page 59 - 1. a large city 2. in a boat 3. a haunted house 4. & 5. Answers may vary.

Page 60 - 1. on a farm belonging to Lola's aunt and uncle 2. a little lamb Answers will vary for questions 3, 4, 5, and 6.

Page 61 - 3,2,1; 3,1,2; 2,3,1

Page 62 - 1. Jack does not like picnics. 2. There are many kinds of trees, too. 3. The library is on the first floor. 4. Some sentences are silly. 5. and looked out the window. 6. It is hard to drive on a snowy road. 7. My dog looks sad. 8. Robins begin to sing.

Page 63 - 1. F 2. T 3. F 4. F 5. T 6. F 7. T 8. T 9. F 10. T 11. T 12. T 13. F 14. T

Page 64 - 2, 4, 7, 9, 10, 11, 12, 13, 14

Page 65 - **A.** 1. hands 2. wheels 3. screen 4. spoons 5. legs **B.** 1. silverware chest 2. chair 3. wagon 4. clock 5. television

Page 66 - **C.** pajamas, book, comb, brush, bathrobe, toothbrush, slippers **D.** 1. Helena and Kay are friends. 2. Sam has a dog. 3. blank

Page 67 - You are learning the code.

Page 68 - Should be shown on graph: Jiro-46 inches, Cindy-44 inches, Marco-42 inches, Celia-38 inches, Sally-36 inches

Page 69 - **A.** 1. e 2. a 3. b 4. c 5. f 6. d **B.** Answers will vary.

Page 70 - **A.** lace, red paper, scissors, crayons, paste, ruler, white paper, yarn Answers will vary for **B,C,D,** and **E.**

Page 71 - **A.** 2, 4, 5 **B.** 4, 2, 3, 1, 5, 6 **C.** Responses will vary.

Page 72 - Responses will vary.

Page 73 - **A.** Mayonnaise already has salt in it. **B.** Answers will vary.

Page 74 - The thief could reach the table, and the parrot could fly. The muffins had little pecks missing, and a parrot pecks. The parrot had crumbs on its feathers. The muffins were hot, and the parrot's mouth hurt.

Page 75 - Answers will vary.

Page 76 - 1. Mr. Larch is collecting bags of leaves. 2. Steve cut his finger on a piece of paper. 3. Marie was in a foreign country and did not speak the language there.

Page 77 - 1. a car that won't run 2. empty plastic bottles 3. newspapers 4. old greeting cards 5. torn shirts 6. old shoes

Page 78 - Sentences will vary.

Page 79 - **A.** 3 dots, line with 1 dot, line with 3 dots, line with 4 dots, 2 lines, 2 lines with 2 dots, 3 lines, 3 lines with 2 dots, 3 lines with 3 dots, 4 lines **B.** 1. c, d 2. b, g 3. a, e 4. f, g, h

Page 80 - **C.** Toys Map: X all departments except Toys **D.** Answers will vary.

Page 81 - 1. No, big-large 2. No, lack 3. Yes 4. Yes 5. No, sing 6. Yes 7. Yes 8. Yes 9. No, this, bus 10. No, rock 11. Yes

Page 82 - Answers will vary.

Page 83 - **A.** 1. fish 2. dog 3. parakeet 4. fish 5. pony 6. Answers will vary. **B.** Answers will vary.

Page 84 - **A.** Answers will vary. 1. a, c, e, f 2. b, c, d, e, g **B.** Answers will vary.

Page 85 - 1. Elisha Otis invented the elevator in 1852. Thank you, Mr. Otis, for inventing the escalator. 2. Pioneers worked hard from morning to night. They usually sat around and played games. 3. Many people remember Ben Franklin because he did an experiment with a kite and lightning. Ben Franklin never did any scientific work, however. 4. Each clown's face is different from all the other clowns. When you go to the circus, all the clowns look alike. 5. Instead of going to school, they stay at home and help with the work. Children in India who do not go to school get to play all day. 6. The Wright brothers were interested in flying. They thought flying was boring.

Page 86 - map, dictionary, encyclopedia, radio, girl from Egypt

Page 87 - Answers may vary. 1. b. He could run an ad in the newspaper. 2. a. He could make a costume that no one else has thought of. 3. c. She could go to bed earlier at night. 4. b. She could watch and listen to find out what he might need or like.

Page 88 - 1. list of materials 2. To make a sand sculpture, you need sand, water, a pail, and a plastic knife or spoon.

Page 89 - **A.** 1. H 2. X 3. X 4. H 5. H 6. X **B.** 1. remind Lois not to litter. 2. go back to the store and trade it for another whistle. 3. try to help the younger boy.

Page 90 - Answers will vary.

Page 91 - Answers may vary. 1. a 2. b 3. b 4. a or b 5. b or c 6. b 7. b 8. c

Page 92 - Answers may vary. 1. content 2. cozy 3. A storm is raging.

Page 93 - **A.** 1. not true 2. true 3. true 4. not true 5. not true **B. Chart:** Fred - black hair, glasses, Ned - dark eyes, black hair, Ed - black hair, Ted - dark eyes, glasses **Pictures:** top left - Fred, top right - Ned, bottom left - Ed, bottom right - Ted

Page 94 - **C.** 1. Underline and circle - Andy was a good sport. 2. Underline - Meg is a caring pet owner. **D.** Answers will vary.

Critical Thinking 3, SV 6214-8